The Newlands and Buttermere Fells

by
Tom Bowker

DALESMAN

First Published in Great Britain 1993 by
Dalesman Publishing Company Limited,
Stable Courtyard, Broughton Hall,
Skipton, North Yorkshire BD23 3AE
Text and drawings © 1993 **Tom Bowker**

ISBN **1 85568 061 0**
Typeset by **Lands Services, East Molesey, Surrey.**
Printed by **Lavenham Press, Lavenham, Suffolk.**

Contents

INTRODUCTION 5

THE NEWLANDS FELLS
Walk 1   The Newlands Horseshoe .... *11.4.0]*..... 7
Walk 2   Dalehead via The Miners' Path 10
Walk 3   Hindscarth and Robinson via Goldscope
          and Scope End 12
Walk 4   The Stonycroft Horseshoe 14
Walk 5   Crag Hill via Tower Ridge 16
Walk 6   The Long Ridge – Rowling End to Grasmoor 17
Walk 7   A Keskadale Horseshoe 20
Walk 8   The Addacomb Round 23

WHINLATTER
Walk 9   The Hobcarton Horseshoe 25

THE BUTTERMERE FELLS
Walk 10   Grasmoor End 28
Walk 11   The Crummock Horseshoe 30
Walk 12   A Different Mosedale Horseshoe 33
Walk 13   The Buttermere Fells 37
Walk 14   The Warnscale Horseshoe 42
Walk 15   The Buttermere Horseshoe 43

MARATHON
Walk 16   The Ennerdale Horseshoe 45

KEY TO MAPS

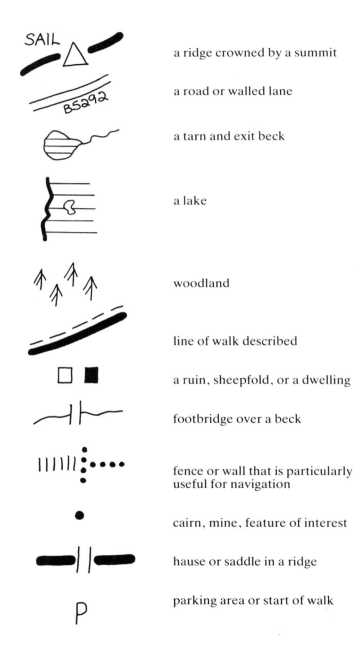

a ridge crowned by a summit

a road or walled lane

a tarn and exit beck

a lake

woodland

line of walk described

a ruin, sheepfold, or a dwelling

footbridge over a beck

fence or wall that is particularly useful for navigation

cairn, mine, feature of interest

hause or saddle in a ridge

parking area or start of walk

INTRODUCTION

THIS fifth book in a series offers walks on the fells that I've loosely termed 'the Newlands Fells' and 'the Buttermere Fells'. The 'Newlands' walks all start and finish at some point in the Newlands Valley, although they may ultimately overlook other valleys. The 'Buttermere' walks do not all necessarily start from Buttermere Village, or the shores of Buttermere itself, but all overlook them for much of their length.

I've always argued that the further west or north-west you travel across Lakeland the more beautiful the valleys and the more shapely and exciting the fells enfolding them. Taste just a handful of the walks described in this book and I'm sure you'll agree that I have a point. Also included, as a bonus for the fellwalker who loves a challenge, is 'The Ennerdale Horseshoe', one of Lakeland's classic 'big walks'. Although not entirely in the area covered by this guidebook, it starts its arduous march over enough of the 'Buttermere' fells to be included. As a guidebook writer I feel myself torn between an eagerness to introduce readers to my beloved Lakeland fells, a natural desire that my books will sell, and a concern that I must accept some blame for the consequent erosion of mountain paths. With the latter in mind I try to diverge from the mountain 'motorways', thus hoping to spread the load a little.

The walks described should be treated with due respect. Boots should be worn and rucksacks should contain waterproofs, spare clothing, map, compass, whistle and survival bag. In winter a torch, balaclava, mittens and some extra food should be added. When snow and ice coat the fells, an ice-axe should be carried. Crampons are becoming more commonly used by fellwalkers, and rightly so. Frequent practice in the use of map and compass make that winter day when their use suddenly becomes vital much less terrifying. Remember the cardinal rule – start using your compass from a point where you know where you are, don't wait until you are lost. Successful navigation through deteriorating conditions adds a bonus to your day and a boost to your confidence. Remember, in an emergency, all becks flow downhill and if followed with care can be fast escape routes in bad weather. Never be afraid to turn back. The fells will still be there next weekend.

Alongside each walk, except for the 'marathon', is a sketch map to be used in conjunction with the text. It is advisable, however, also to carry the relevant sheet of the 1:25000 The English Lakes Outdoor Leisure Maps. All the place names in the text refer to an edition of these maps. The mileages and heights of ascent are approximate and 'left' or 'right' refers to a physical feature as if facing it. Parking details are as per the maps, local authorities and tradition up to press, but are always liable to change. Limited space means I have to choose between detailed route descriptions, incidental information, and detailed description of views. I tend to be niggardly with the latter, feeling it's useful for walkers to attempt to orientate the view to their map.

The only way to learn about the fells is to be out regularly in all conditions. There will be times when you are frightened and times when you are physically exhausted. Ironically, these are the days that live most vividly in the memory and when you learn something about the mountains. Don't forget that it's a game, it's fun, it's adventure. For the fellwalker, given reasonable fitness and equipment, using his/her commonsense, the dangers are more apparent than real. Statistically, you are probably in more danger in your home or on your journey to and from the fells.

The Lakeland fells have become inextricably woven into the weft of my life. My addiction to climbing them led to love, marriage and fatherhood, and innumerable friendships. They stimulated my interest in writing and are the bedrock of its continuing development. They have given me untold days of rewarding physical endeavour, good company, and wonderment at the beauty seen. If this booklet should bring such pleasures to any who read it I will be content. Happy walking!

Tom Bowker

THE NEWLANDS FELLS

Walk 1

Distance 12 miles
4000 feet of ascent

The Newlands Horseshoe

Arguably the finest of all the popular Lakeland 'horseshoes'. The walking is challenging and the constantly changing views are breathtakingly lovely. Try and save this one for a fine clear day.

Parking: Gutherscale car park (GR 246211). Fork right from the hair-pin below the Catbells on the Portinscale – Grange-in-Borrowdale road. If full, park in the trees below the hair-pin or in lay-bys on the roadside some distance above it.

START up the path at the corner of the hairpin where the lane to the carpark forks off. More little boys and girls must have been cajoled, carried or dragged to the top of the Catbells than to any other Lakeland top. Both my daughters 'bagged' it early, and we have a photograph of my eldest daughter being fed her 'pobs' on the lower summit. This summer I plan to snap her feeding my grandson in exactly the same spot.

Mart Bield, 1479 feet, the highest 'Catbell', is, in shape, every inch a mountain. Were it possible to inject it with two thousand feet of Borrowdale Volcanic it would become a prized scalp for the 'peak bagger'. Descend onto the saddle of Hause Gate and climb up the far slope onto the broad ridge of Maiden Moor. Leave the worn path and wander along the fell rim to your right for the spectacular views back onto the Catbells and across a gulf of Lakeland air towards Hindscarth, a handsome peak, yet to be 'bagged'. The great fan of grey slate spoil spilled at the foot of Hindscarth marks the site of the defunct Goldscope Mine (see Walk 3).

When the ridge narrows (Narrow Moor), fork left to a cairn crowning a rocky viewpoint over the verdant Jaws of Borrowdale. Return to the main path and head down into the dip below High Spy. Scramble onto the rocks to the right of the dip for a spectacular 'bird's-eye' view into the rugged head of Newlands. Pick out the old miners' track zig-zagging up onto the precipitous north flank of Dalehead, which gives an interesting and uncrowded ascent (see Walk 2).

From the handsome cairn crowning High Spy, 2143 feet, descend south down the stony twisting path into the hollow cupping Dalehead Tarn. Cross the outlet beck, climb between outcrops and swing right to a sheepfold tucked under a crag on the shore of the tarn, a pleasant spot for lunch.

Continue along the path to the right of the tarn which steepens considerably before easing out onto a shoulder overlooking Dalehead's steep northern flank. (Walk 2 also emerges onto this shoulder). A short steep climb up and around the rim of the fell brings you to the fine cairn crowning Dalehead, 2470 feet, the monarch of the Newlands Horseshoe. Dalehead is a fine viewpoint. To the south the elegant cone of Great Gable is easily identifiable. To its left are the high jumbled mass of the Scafells, with Esk Pike and Bowfell further left, beyond the saddle of Esk Hause. To the right of Gable are the tableland summit of Kirkfell, the gap of Black Sail Pass, and the high dome of Pillar. In the foreground, below Pillar, are the Buttermere trio of High Crag, High Stile and Red Pike. Rising immediately below you, out of the defile of Honister Pass, is Fleetwith Pike, with Haystacks peeking over its shoulder. Below the fell's airy north flank the narrow bare reaches of Newlands stretch away to more pastoral lowlands and the distant roofs of Keswick.

Descend just north of west along the fell rim down the rocky but somewhat grandiosely christened Hindscarth Edge, the rocks of which are spiked with solitary and ancient fence posts. Buttermere now gleams darkly in the depths to your left. In the grassy dip below Hindscarth a fainter path forks right. Turn along this onto a slanting grassy climb across the east flank of Hindscarth to reach the summit cairn at 2385 feet.

Now make a slanting descent across the fell's easy-angled west flank onto the saddle, crowned by a wood and wire fence, below Robinson. Turn right and climb the worn path alongside the fence onto the summit ridge of Robinson. Leave the fence here and walk right to shortly reach the cairn, balanced on a protruding rib of slaty rock, crowning Robinson, 2417 feet. The fell was named after a local Tudor entrepreneur who was quick to grasp the opportunities offered by the Dissolution of the Monasteries, for the monks held much of Lakeland. The view over Crummock Water, far Loweswater, and the peaks jostling around Grasmoor is very fine. A bonus on a clear day is the northern prow of the Isle of Man thrusting over the shoulder of Red Pike.

Descend the cairned path, bearing gradually north-easterly and subsequently along the rim of the fell's precipitous north west flank. Two steep, slaty rock steps lead down onto the grassy ridge of High Snab Bank (Under icy conditions these rock steps could become extremely hazardous. Under such circumstances it could be advisable to climb back a little way then descend into Littledale and follow the path leading out of this valley, down past the old mine reservoir and on to Low High Snab). Given dry conditions,

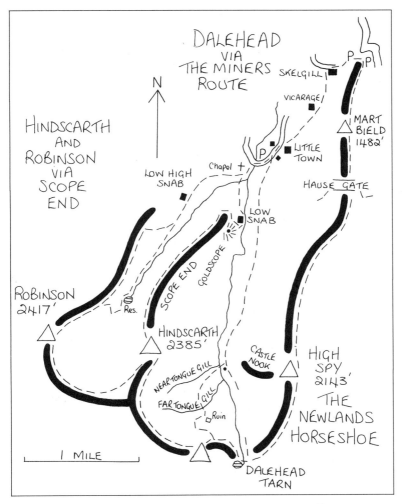

DALEHEAD
VIA
THE MINERS
ROUTE

HINDSCARTH
AND
ROBINSON
VIA
SCOPE
END

SKELGILL

VICARAGE

MART
BIELD
1482'

LOW HIGH
SNAB

Chapel +

P

LITTLE
TOWN

HAUSE GATE

LOW
SNAB

ROBINSON
2417'

Res.

SCOPE END

GOLDSCOPE

HINDSCARTH
2385'

CASTLE
NOOK

HIGH
SPY
2143'

NEAR TONGUE GILL

FAR TONGUE GILL

Ruin

THE
NEWLANDS
HORSESHOE

1 MILE

DALEHEAD
TARN

the rock steps add an exciting bonus to the day. A fingerpost on
the crest of High Snab Bank points you right down a steep grassy
path that ends at the entrance to a walled track leading to Low
High Snab Farm. Follow the tarmac to a T-junction just beyond
Newlands Church. Turn right over Chapel Bridge and climb up the
road into the hamlet of Little Town. Go through the buildings then
turn right along a path that bridges Yewthwaite Gill and meanders
pleasantly across the meadows to Skelgill Farm. On emerging onto
the tarmac turn right up to a gate which leads onto a track leading
down to Gutherscale car park.

Dalehead via The Miners' Path

Walk up Newlands and you pass through fell-fringed meadows into a crag and scree-lined defile which funnels you into the splendid corrie below Dalehead. Dalehead's precipitous northern flank is then climbed by a spiralling path, redolent of the Alps, initially built by miners. The return along the popular path past Dalehead Tarn and over the benign switchbacks of High Spy, Maiden Moor, and Catbells, with lovely Lakeland unrolling away below your toecaps, is a delight.

Parking: As for Walk 1.

WALK up the lane from the car-park to a gate. Go through it and down past Skelgill Farm house then turn immediately left, by a horse trough, to a gate. Go through the gate and behind the farmhouse, taking care not to be garrotted by the washing line, to a gate/stile. Beyond this, follow a pleasant path across the meadows. To your right looms Causey Pike, with Sail and Crag Hill piling up behind it. Left of them, across the defile of Rigg Beck, is conical Ard Crags, and further left the saddle of Newlands Hause, beyond which, out of the depths of Buttermere, peeps High Stile. Left of Newlands Hause rise Robinson and Hindscarth, both throwing elegant ridges down into Newlands.

Beyond The Vicarage the path becomes a walled lane which joins the public road at Little Town. Turn left and walk through the hamlet. Just before the road drops steeply fork left through a gate, signposted 'Newlands' on its far side. A rough, former mining track, leads easily up the narrowing valley. You can pick out the line of the miners' path as the north flank looms closer, and higher into the sky, with every step. To your right, dwarfing the roofs of Low Snab Farm, which, incidentally, offers one of the tastiest 'cuppas' in Lakeland, are the pale and monstrous spoil heaps of the now defunct Goldscope Mine. (See Walk 3).

When the rocky spur of Castle Nook is rounded, the path divides by a cairn. Take the lower path down to the bank of Newlands Beck. Across the beck the start of the miners' path is clearly defined slanting up from the mouth of Near Tongue Gill. As you climb, absorb the atmosphere of this fine corrie, filled with the brooding light common to all north facing combes, and rimmed by crags, several of which are steep and stern enough to have rock climbs 'chalked' upon them. After crossing the mouth of slabby, deeply-cleft Far Tongue Gill, delightful grassy spirals lead up to a bouldery shelf crowned by a ruined miners' workshop. On our last visit the shelf was sown with starry saxifrage and the delectable eyebright.

Climb a stony path behind the workshop which slants leftwards across the steep fellside, crossing the spoil heap of a blocked mine shaft. At over two thousand feet above sea level it must have been one of the highest workings in Lakeland, exposed at times to some pretty foul weather. Passing this way in our designer walking gear and boots, ample food and drink in our packs, is one thing. Climbing up here daily in cheap boots and homespun clothing, all possibly sodden with rain or snow, hunger gnawing in your belly, to toil day long in the dark slimy guts of the hill, was another.

The final section of the path crosses a steep grassy slope before emerging on to a shoulder and a junction with the worn 'Newlands Horseshoe' path. (Given hard snow or icy conditions it would be advisable to carry an ice axe or wear crampons on the miners' path. The final steep grassy slope is poised above crags and a slip here in winter could have serious consequences.) On the shoulder, turn right up the worn path to shortly reach the cairn crowning Dalehead, 2470 feet. (For aspects of the view see Walk 1.)

Return down to the shoulder and continue down the worn path to Dalehead Tarn. Walk to the left of the tarn, past a sheepfold, then left between outcrops and down to and across the infant Newlands Beck. The rest of your return route back to your car requires little description. An eroded path along a well-defined ridge makes for easy navigation and therefore little distraction from superb views. Beyond Dalehead Tarn the path twists stonily up to the handsome cairn crowning High Spy, 2143 feet. Move left for a 'bird's-eye' view of the miners' path, with the jumbled, shadow-cleft cones and spires of the Grasmoor and Coledale fells rising beyond the blued depths of Newlands. Beyond High Spy the ridge undulates down on to Maiden Moor, 1889 feet, then more steeply down on to Hause Gate. A final climb leads on to the invariably crowded cone of Cat Bells, 1478 feet, where it's obligatory to sit awhile and feast on the beauty of Derwentwater, and its flotilla of wooded isles, before descending leisurely to your car.

Hindscarth and Robinson
via Goldscope and Scope End

*From Little Town, imposing, triple-peaked Scope End looks decidedly
'interesting'. Proving less difficult to climb in fact than it appears in
form, this ridge nevertheless offers another entertaining approach to
the fine fells encircling the head of Newlands. For those interested in
the industrial history of Lakeland there is an added bonus in being
able to explore, with due caution, the spoil heaps and adits of the
derelict Goldscope Mine.*

*Parking: Take the minor road from Stair to Little Town. There is
limited parking on the verges at the bottom of the steep hill beyond
Little Town. (GR 232194.)*

FOLLOW the road over Chapel Bridge and turn left through a
gate. By Newlands Church fork left along a farm road. Cross a
packhorse bridge and continue ahead to reach Low Snab Farm.
Go through the farmyard to a gate.

Piled up beyond the gate are the massive spoil heaps of the
defunct Goldscope Mine. 'Goldscope' has nothing to do with gold
but is a corruption of 'Gottes Gab' or 'God's Gift', the name given
by the sixteenth-century immigrant German miners who worked
the rich veins of lead and copper, thirteen and nine feet thick. The
Germans were skilled, travelled, and highly paid compared to the
local peasantry. The pack trains that took refined ore out over the
fells brought back wines, spices, linen bedcovers and feather beds.
No wonder local girls were beguiled into often bigamous marriages.
During the Second World War disgruntled British servicemen
referred to their American allies as 'overpaid, oversexed, and over
here'. Elizabethan Cumbrian males probably expressed similar
disenchantment with the Germans for there were some ugly scenes
and at least one murder. For a time the immigrants were lodged on
Derwent Isle for their own safety. Eventually they became accepted,
and between 1565 and 1584, 176 children of German fathers were
registered at Crosthwaite Church. Beck, Moser, Calvert, Raisley
and Caryus are just a handful of the anglicized German names
surviving in Cumbria.

Above the spoil heaps the entrances to the 'adits', or horizontal
passages, slant up the fellside. These apparently followed the
copper vein to meet up with the lead vein deep inside the ridge.
Scope End is pierced from either flank and in its stony bowels, I'm

told, is a 'stope', a kind of shaft or ledged working face, over five hundred feet deep.

Climb right from the gate, away from the spoil heap and along-side a wall/fence, towards the foot of the ridge. Near a 'private' sign on the wall/fence, fork left. A steep path, with some rocky steps, leads eventually onto the crest of the ridge. Fine walking follows along an undulating, safe, but pleasantly airy ridge. Graceful Hindscarth beckons ahead and all around 'every prospect pleases'. A final steepish climb leads to a handsome wind shelter just below the cairn crowning the 2385 foot summit.

From the summit, now follow the directions given in Walk 1 from 'Now make a slanting descent across the fell's easy-angled west flank' to 'Turn right over Chapel Bridge' to return to your car.

13

The Stonycroft Horseshoe

Barrow, Stile End and Outerside, encircled and dominated as they are by the higher peaks of the popular Coledale Horseshoe, tend to get neglected, which is a pity, for Barrow and Outerside are amongst the finest minor fells (under two thousand feet) in Lakeland, and worth the effort. Combined with Scar Crags and Causey Pike they provide an entertaining and fairly amiable 'horseshoe' around the Stonycroft Gill. A useful reconnaissance walk for those contemplating attempting 'scrambly' Walk 5, or more arduous Walk 8, or both.

Parking: In Braithwaite, follow the 'Newlands' sign left, over the narrow bridge. Ignore the 'Swinside' fork, and when the wood on your right ends, beyond a cattle grid, look for a space to park on the grass verge on your right. (GR 234224.)

WALK up the road, past a memorial seat, to where a path signposted 'Public Bridleway – Braithwaite' slants up the fellside to your right. Follow this. When Braithwaite comes into view below and ahead, with Bassenthwaite Lake gleaming beyond, the path forks. Follow the upper path to a junction with the path climbing Barrow's north-east ridge. Turn left up this. A straightforward and grassy plod now leads to a dip bearing traces of past mining.

Barrow's narrow and heathery summit beckons ahead, with Causey Pike's dimpled crest and the notched ridge of Scar Crags looming above and beyond. The gap to the right of Scar Crag is Sail Hause, dominated by the dome of Sail. To your right, Stile End and Outerside beckon in the foreground. Beyond them bulky Crag Hill and graceful Grisedale Pike, divided by the saddle of Coledale Hause, dominate the head of Coledale. The Cistercian monks of the 14th century drained 'Husaker Tarn' in order to create their 'Neulandes'. The name and the site linger on in Uzzicar Farm at the foot of the steep slope to your left.

From Barrow top the path bears right and down into the heathery saddle of Barrow Door. A path linking Braithwaite and Stonycroft Gill crosses the saddle. Cross this path and climb rightwards up onto the rounded summit of Stile End, the most innocuous of your trio. From Stile End head south-westerly across the boggy saddle of Low Moss towards the inviting shape of Outerside. The path is indistinct at times but improves as Outerside is approached. A final steep pull brings you onto the pleasant grassy summit ridge crowned by a cairn at its far end.

Because it is tucked deep into the heart of the Coledale Horseshoe the views from Outerside are restricted. I personally find compensation in the intimate detail revealed in the mountain architecture of its loftier neighbours, particularly the rugged north-east flank of Crag Hill looming ahead. Close inspection of this face will reveal a broad rocky rib running up the centre of it, and from the foot of this rib a natural shelf climbing diagonally rightwards to an obvious nick in the skyline. Mr. Wainright has christened the rib 'Tower Ridge' and the natural line 'Shelf Route'. Both are entertaining, especially under snow. Below the western rim of Outerside lie the ramshackle buildings of Force Crag Mine. Barytes was mined here and the mine has been sporadically operational until quite recently. Above the buildings Pudding Beck spills creamily over Force Crag.

Now descend left, south, to join, near a sheepfold, the rough former miners' track above Stonycroft Gill. Turn right and follow this over the broad saddle of High Moss and leftwards onto the steep, shaly fellside overlooking Long Comb. Climb the path slanting across this fellside to reach Sail Hause. Having now gained the higher rim of the Coledale Horseshoe your view becomes more wide-ranging.

Turn left and climb the somewhat boggy path leading to the summit of Scar Crags, 2204 feet. The slope to your right falls steeply into the valley of the Rigg Beck. The rather stunted-looking trees clinging to the slopes below you are sessile oaks, puportedly one of the surviving areas of 'relict' or native woodland. Beyond Scar Crags a dip leads onto the knobbly summit of Causey Pike, 2089 feet. Seen from Keswick, or the shores of Derwentwater, cocky Causey Pike offers a challenge that lures many a 'non-fellwalker'. Though they get this far and no further, the scramble up its rocky cap, the sense of space and the glorious prospect probably converts more than a few to the great game of climbing mountains.

From Causey Pike a steep rocky descent leads eventually onto easier ground and a path fork. The left fork offers the shortest and easiest descent. If you continue along the ridge to Rowling End, however, you retain the splendid views which are worth the few twinges your knees might suffer on the steep descent from the end of the ridge. Both routes meet the road near Stonycroft Bridge. Turn left to reach your car.

Walk 5

Distance 8½ miles
3500 feet of ascent
OR Distance 11 miles
4300 feet of ascent

Crag Hill via Tower Ridge

For those who have already tasted the pleasures of the Coledale Horseshoe and fancy something with a taste of 'mountaineering' about it, this is an enjoyable outing. Under winter conditions Tower Ridge must be taken seriously and the proper kit for the job carried. Bearing that in mind, it is an enjoyable and relatively easy rock scramble.

Parking: As for Walk 4.

FOLLOW the directions given in Walk 4 as far as the summit of Outerside, and then read the description of Tower Ridge and Shelf Route as given there.

Now descend south-westerly into the hollow of Long Comb. Cross the head of Birkthwaite Beck and contour around the base of the north-east ridge of Sail into the combe beyond. Climb right to join the Shelf Route path. Follow it until you are below the rocky tors of Tower Ridge, which looms quite impressively from this angle. Leave the path and climb up to the foot of the rocks. Climb the ridge, picking whichever way gives you the most fun.

We once climbed it when the ridge was plastered with Easter snow. Below us a helicopter 'buzzed' the combe, the echoes of its rotor-blades 'thwack-thwacking' unnervingly around us. A holiday granted for a Royal Wedding gave us, in contrast, a delightful scramble up sun-warmed rock.

Climb left along the summit ridge to the trig-point crowning Crag Hill, 2752 feet. Return pleasantly to your car over Sail, Scar Crags, and Causey Pike. If, however, you are feeling fit and have time to spare, descend WSW to the tiny pools crowning the grassy saddle below Grasmoor. Climb beyond them to 'bag' this fine fell. Return to the pools then climb south-easterly to reach the summit cairn of Wandope, perched on the airy rim of Addacomb Hole. Now follow the rim of Addacomb Hole back up on to the summit of Crag Hill and return to your car over Sail, Scar Crags and Causey Pike. (Should you require a more detailed description of the options detailed above, after 'Crag Hill, 2752 feet.', study Walks 6 and 8.

The Long Ridge –
Rowling End to Grasmoor

Quality ridge-walking demands certain criteria. A fine sense of space to either hand, wide flung and ever-changing views, and the constant challenge of yet another summit beckoning ahead. Walk from Rowling End to Grasmoor and you'll find all there in abundance. Add Wandope and a little used descent into a lonely high corrie and you will have enjoyed yet another 'great' Lakeland day.

Parking: As for Walks 4 and 5.

WALK up the road to Stonycroft Bridge. Cross the bridge, turn right, climb past a seat and attack the path twisting up the towering prow of Rowling End. It's a lung-bursting start, with a couple of soul-destroying false summits, but the effort is worthwhile. Once on the crest, you'll soon forget your aching legs and pounding heartbeat as your eyes and mind soak in the gorgeous views.

Continue along the ridge and then more steeply up to the foot of the summit rocks of Causey Pike, 2035 feet. Their ascent proves easier than might be expected on first sight. Continue along the ridge to the dip below Scar Crags. The summit ridge of Scar Crags, 2205 feet, is broader than it would appear from the valley and surprisingly boggy. Look over the left-hand rim to see a plantation of stunted trees clinging to the fellside. These are the Birkrigg Oaks, reputedly one of the surviving stands of 'relict', or original, woodland.

Beyond Scar Crags cross the dip of Sail Hause and attack the steep eroded path leading on to the grassy summit dome of Sail, 2530 feet. Walk right to the tiny cairn, then past it to the fell rim for a fine view over Coledale. At the foot of the steep shaly south-east flank of Grisedale Pike stand the disused workshops of Force Crag Mine. Barytes was mined here until well after the Second World War. When gripped in ice, the waterfall that spills down the massive vegetated Force Crag becomes a much-prized ascent for climbers.

Beyond Sail, the ridge dips again, becoming narrower and rockier before curving up on to the grassy summit dome, crowned by a trig-point, of Crag Hill, 2753 feet. The west flank of Crag Hill, in contrast to its precipitous and craggy eastern flank, is broad, easy-angled grassland sloping into an upland valley that tilts northwards

17

onto Coledale Hause. The sprawling bulk of Grasmoor dominates the far side of this valley. In contrast to Crag Hill the topography of Grasmoor is reversed. Its eastern flank is largely grassy and easy-angled, whilst its western flank tumbles down on to Lanthwaite Green in a frozen cascade of crag, gully and scree fan.

Follow a path west-south-westerly down to the head of the valley to where paths meet near some small pools. Climb west-north-westerly up a worn path to a cairn. Beyond the cairn follow a path cutting across the rim of Grasmoor's steep shaly south flank. Far below lies the ancient battleground of Rannerdale (see Walk 11). Cross a rise on to the turfy summit plateau to shortly reach the cairns and capacious wind shelter crowning Grasmoor's 2791 foot summit. Walk the few steps to the fell rim for the 'birds-eye' view of Buttermere and Crummock Water.

Return by the same route to the pools. Now climb south-easterly (or diagonally right from the path you descended from Crag Hill), up easy grass, to reach the cairn crowning the airy prow of Wandope, 2533 feet. Because of its position, jutting out over a deep valley, Wandope is a fine viewpoint. Rising immediately in the foreground are the fells forming the Newlands Horseshoe (Walk 1), with a magnificent jumble of hills, ranging from Pillar to Helvellyn, rising beyond. This is a good spot to orientate your map to the view. Below your toe-caps, the surprisingly razor-edged crest of the Ard Crags-Knott Rigg ridge (Walk 7), rises out of the depths of the Sail Beck.

Descend the steep prow overlooking this valley, down a faint path twisting around jutting rocks. (Under hard snow, or ice, this section could be potentially hazardous if you were without crampons or ice-axe). To your left is Addacomb Hole, an unfrequented hanging valley which would be an ideal site for an undisturbed high camp or bivouac. The ridge eventually loses definition, sinking into the steep brackeny fellside. To your left the beck whose source was a messy sponge in the bowl of Addacomb Hole now sports a fine waterfall. Descend to a crossing path near where it fords this beck (Addacomb Beck). Notice the crumbling stonework hereabouts, indicative of former mining. Look back up for an interesting view of Wandope, Addacomb Hole, and the waterfall spilling from it.

Follow the path across the beck and diagonally up and around the flank of Sail. Ignore the path forking left up to Sail Hause, and continue on to the grassy saddle at the head of Sail Beck. Follow the path across the saddle and down into the valley of the Rigg Beck. Keep your eyes open for a fork in the path. Take the right fork and follow it down to reach the road near where it bridges the Rigg Beck. Turn left along the road back to your car.

On a recent descent of this path we paused to watch two hares cavort at high speed up and down the fellside across the Rigg Beck. Simultaneously, two buzzards patrolled the crest of the ridge above them. Neither pair appeared aware of, or were deliberately ignoring, each other. Perhaps the raptors had declared a truce in Newlands that lovely spring afternoon. Clinging, with a grating chitter, to a nearby bracken stalk was a preening stonechat. Such unexpected glimpses of wildlife add a delightful bonus to days on the Lakeland fells.

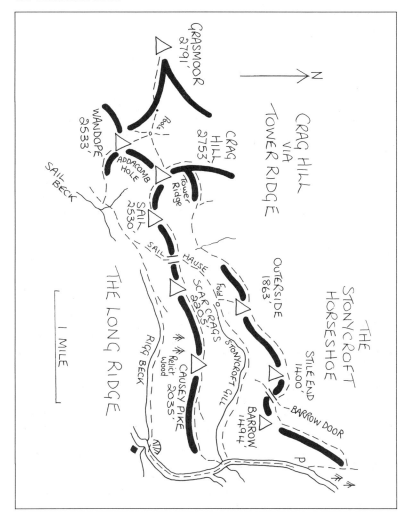

A Keskadale Horseshoe

*Though squeezed between the more glamorous Newlands and
Coledale 'horseshoes', this is nevertheless a worthy outing for its
own sake. Also useful for reconnaissance if you have your eye on
either of these walks as it offers unusual views of both.*

*Parking: In a disused quarry, on the right, just before the Braithwaite
to Buttermere road crosses the Rigg Beck. (GR 229202.)*

FOLLOW the footpath along the right bank of Rigg Beck. When
the wall on the far bank of the beck turns uphill cross the beck and
climb alongside this wall onto the crest of a ridge. Turn right and
climb along the ridge, and over the rocks of Aikin Knott, ultimately
to reach the cairn crowning the summit of Ard Crags, 1906 feet.
(Aikin Knott is reputedly the last resting place of Jarl Hakon, a
Cumbrian war-chief slain at the battle of Rannerdale, see Walk 11).

The elegant Ard Crags-Knott Rigg ridge has a tendency to be
ignored because it rises in the shadow of higher fells, which is a
pity, for its long crest is airy, in the pleasant rather than the
frightening sense of the word, and a fascinating viewpoint. Below,
clinging to a fold in the southern flank of Ard Crags, are the
Keskadale Oaks, arguably one of the surviving areas of 'relict', or
native woodland.

In the dip beyond Ard Crags, a tiny tarn is passed before the
climb up onto the double-topped summit of Knott Rigg, 1824
feet. Descend the ridge beyond to reach the road where it crosses
Newlands Hause. Ahead, and below, as you descend, lie the roofs
of Buttermere, a darkly glinting segment of Crummock Water, and
the silver thread of Sour Milk Gill spilling through Red Pike's
sombre skirt of trees.

Cross the road and spend some time enjoying the fine cascades
of Moss Force. Follow the path climbing steeply up the right edge
of the crag over which Moss Beck spills. Eventually, a boggy groove
leads on to easier ground above the crags. Below, to your left, the
bleak uplands of Keskadale stretch away towards more verdant
Newlands, with a glimpse of distant Derwentwater. Ahead of you
the summit dome of Robinson looms above Buttermere Moss.
Turn right and climb gently south-westerly up a faint grassy path,
following firm ground between the Moss and the rim of the fellside
falling down to the road. Ahead rises the subsidiary summit of
High Snockrigg. Shortly, the path from Buttermere joins in up

a groove on your right. Below, to your right, the knobbly crest of Rannerdale Knotts is etched against the glittery surface of Crummock Water, with Loweswater and the far Solway Firth gleaming beyond.

The path now curves left, south-easterly to east, attempting to avoid the squelchy hazards of Buttermere Moss. For the most part it succeeds, but the Moss spreads its swampy tentacles wide, and before you reach the large cairn at the foot of the summit dome you will be lucky if you have escaped unscathed. From the cairn, climb steeply leftwards up a worn slaty groove. This final climb is not one for indulging in chatter, and you'll be puffing by the time you reach the summit cairn of Robinson, 2417 feet, perched on its slaty outcrop.

Now read and follow the description given in Walk 1 from "The fell was named " to "beyond Newlands Church".

Now turn left and follow the narrow road up to a junction with the Braithwaite-Buttermere road near a purple house, and close to your car.

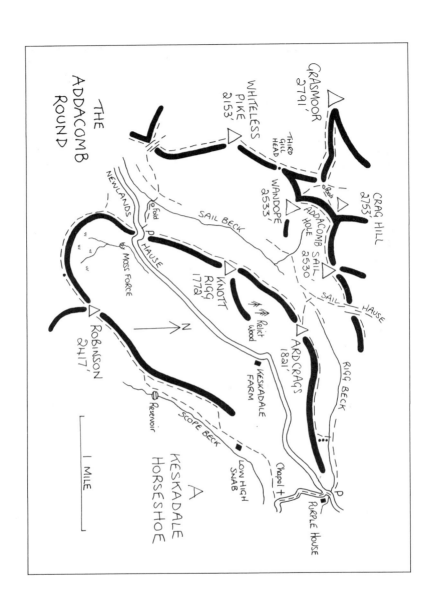

THE ADDACOMB ROUND

GRASMOOR 2791'

WHITELESS PIKE 2153'

THIRD GILL HEAD

CRAG HILL 2753'

WANDOPE 2533'

ADDACOMB SAIL, HOLE 2530'

NEWLANDS

fold

SAIL BECK

SAIL HAUSE

MOSS FORCE

HAUSE

KNOTT RIGG 1772'

Relict Wood

ARDCRAGS 1821'

RIGG BECK

N

ROBINSON 2417'

KESKADALE FARM

Reservoir

SCOPE BECK

LOW HIGH SNAB

Chapel +

P
PURPLE HOUSE

1 MILE

A KESKADALE HORSESHOE

22

The Addacomb Round

Every mountain area has its 'classic' walks. Walks that have been praised in books and articles, and in bars, bothies, hostels, climbing club huts, campsites, or wherever mountain folk gather. Obviously guidebook writers must include the 'classics' but I believe that they should also use their imagination and experience to offer some less well-known but equally interesting variations on a popular theme. It also eases the wear and tear on the popular walks. So, in this book, I have ignored the Coledale Horseshoe but offer other approaches to, and explorations of, its splendid tops and ridges.

Parking: In the lay-bys on the summit of Newlands Hause. (GR 193176.)

DESCEND the right bank of Swinside Gill to its confluence with the Sail Beck near a small sheepfold. As you descend, scrutinise the fellside rising beyond the beck. You seek a path crossing this fellside, above and parallel to the Sail Beck, and a path forking and climbing leftwards from this path. Cross Sail Beck and climb the fellside to the fork described. Climb the leftward slanting path to emerge on to the narrow col at the head of Rannerdale. Beyond Rannerdale gleam Crummock Water, Loweswater, and the distant Solway Firth. (See Walk 11 regarding the Battle of Rannerdale.) Look left for a splendid view over Buttermere, ringed by excitingly cleft fells.

Climb right from the col. The steep twists do ease but stiffen again before you eventually puff up to the cairn crowning Whiteless Pike, 2159 feet. Look right, down on to the grassy blade of the Ard Crags-Knott Rigg ridge, the splendid finale to your expedition. Descend into a dip and climb the narrow ridge which rejoices in the grandiose title of Whiteless Edge. This 'edge' would need to be plastered thick with snow and ice before it really got scary. Walk past the cairn crowning Third Gill Head and follow the path curving leftwards above the fell rim to a junction of paths, near some tiny pools, on the grassy saddle between Grasmoor and Crag Hill.

Turn left and climb a worn path to a cairn. Continue, along a path cutting across the rim of the steep shaly south flank of Grasmoor, to cross a rise and shortly reach the cairns and substantial wind shelter crowning Grasmoor, 2795 feet. Walk the few steps to the rim for a 'bird's-eye' view of Crummock Water. To the south-east, the long cloven Bowfell-Scafell skyline, with Gable's cone superimposed darkly upon it, is particularly eye-catching. Retrace your steps to the pools on the saddle then climb grassy slopes south-easterly to reach the cairn crowning the airy prow of Wandope, 2532 feet. As you climb, look right, between Grasmoor and Third Gill Head, possibly to spot the Isle of Man floating above the flattish summit of Great Bourne and the tiny cone of Floutern Cop.

Turn left, down then up, around the rim of Addacomb Hole, a sliced-off volcano stuck on the side of Crag Hill. A pity it's not blessed with a tarn. At the highest point of the rim walk left to reach the trig-point crowning Crag Hill, 2752 feet. Descend easterly, down and along The Scar, a narrow rocky ridge that could require some care under winter conditions. A short climb then leads on to the grassy dome of Sail, 2536 feet. Walk left to the tiny cairn then beyond it for a fine view over Coledale. Coledale means 'valley of the charcoal burners, or colliers' which suggests that centuries ago this great bare bowl of a valley was thick with forest, which was plundered to feed the fiery maw of the miners' smelters.

Return and descend the worn path on to Sail Hause, with Derwentwater peeking around either side of the knobbly crest of Causey Pike, below and ahead. Turn right, on the saddle of Sail Hause, and descend a narrow path through the heather. Below you lies a grassy saddle. At a convenient point leave the path and descend through the heather on to this saddle. Cross it and climb the steep grass slope beyond to eventually emerge on to the crest of Ard Crags, 1906 feet, near its cairn. It's a tough climb at this stage of the walk but adds much of interest if you feel up to it. (If you don't feel up to it simply follow the path from Sail Hause down to a junction with a crossing path. Turn right and follow this path down into the valley of the Sail Beck to a junction with your outward route at the confluence with Swinside Gill.)

From Ard Crags, turn right and follow the ridge over Knott Rigg, 1824 feet, and on down to Newlands Hause. It's a lovely finish, giving exciting views and delightful going, to a splendid walk. Well worth the extra effort.

WHINLATTER

Distance 7 miles
2100 feet of ascent

The Hobcarton Horseshoe

A somewhat tortuous start through forest, but once the crest is gained yet another delightful ridge walk unfolds ahead. At first glance, the summit ridge of Hopegill Head may give pause for thought, but what you don't fancy you can easily avoid. Think twice, however, if the mountain is sheathed in hard snow or ice and you have neither the gear or experience needed.

Parking: In the Visitor Centre Car Park on the crest of Whinlatter Pass (GR 207245).

WALK back on to the road and turn right. Walk just under a mile down the road to a forest road entrance on your left. Turn into the entrance and then almost immediately right at a junction of forest roads. Climb over a rise then go down to a concrete bridge over the Hobcarton Gill, passing the entrances to forest roads 35 and 36. Rising above the trees to your left is Ladyside Pike, crowned by its sizeable cairn. Cross the bridge and climb a forest road zig-zagging up right then left to a junction. Ignore the forest road numbered 37 climbing right and continue leftwards, or straight ahead as it may seem to you, to eventually reach a gate at the edge of the forest.

Go through the gate and a ramshackle sheep pen and follow a faint path slanting across the fellside towards and past an old sheepfold. Just beyond the sheepfold look to your right to see a path slanting right up the steep fellside. Climb this, passing through the weathered husks of ancient trees, to reach a fence corner. Climb over the fence to your left, then directly up the grassy fellside ahead, ignoring faint paths bearing left and right alongside the fence.

Continue climbing, passing the occasional rusting iron fencepost, until the angle eases and the slope descends to abut an old wall and a wood and wire fence. Below now, chequered fields unroll to the rim of Cumbria and the grey waters of the Solway Firth. Turn left and follow a path alongside the wall/fence to reach a stile in a crossing fence. Cross this and climb the steepish grass ridge that brings you to the handsome cairn crowning Ladyside Pike, 2306 feet.

The ridge ahead dips then rises steeply in challenging, some may think threatening, rocky ramparts to the summit of Hopegill Head.

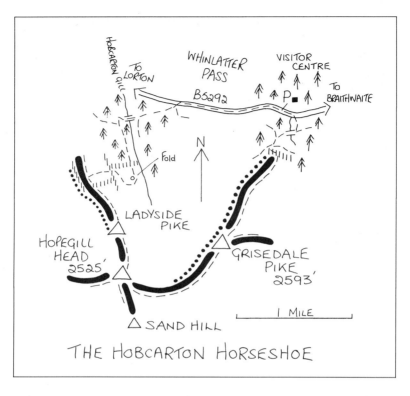

THE HOBCARTON HORSESHOE

Don't worry, its bark is worse than its bite. Descend easily into the dip and on up to the first slaty rock tower. All apparent difficulties can be avoided by simply moving to the right, eventually to climb a shallow groove, or fault line, which leads easily to the summit. If the rock is dry, however, scramble along the crest and keep left and as close as you can bear to the airy rim of Hobcarton Crag. This will lead you on to a slabby platform and across a substantial notch to a delightful finish up a narrow rocky ridge on to the summit of Hopegill Head, 2525 feet. A proper mountain top this, a rocky perch thrust over gulfs of Cumbrian air. Southwards, the Wandope cone divides the brawny shapes of Crag Hill and Grasmoor. In a gap to the left of Crag Hill, spot the blue distant cone of Langdale's Pike O'Stickle. Down to your right, Crummock Water glitters in the dark V of Gasgale Gill.

Descend left, south-easterly at first, then gradually swinging east, along the path following the rim of the fell, or sometimes just below it, into a dip. Take care hereabouts, in winter conditions, for the ground falls precipitously away below the path. From a rocky pulpit on the rim of the dip, look back with awe at the spectacular skyline of the ridge you have just climbed and its equally spectacular position poised over Hobcarton Crag. Despite its dizzying splendour Hobcarton Crag fails to attract rock-climbers because its rock is too friable. It does, however, attract kamikaze botanists for the rare Red Alpine Catchfly, Viscaria Alpina, has bloomed in its grotty crags and gullies.

Climb out of the dip alongside an old wall. Follow it over a rocky hump bestriding the ridge. Descend shortly beyond before following the wall up the shaly and steepening ridge that leads on to the summit of Grisedale Pike, 2593 feet. It's been my experience to find this summit one of the windiest in Lakeland. I'm not alone in this. One winter day a friend of mine was crossing it when he was hit by a blast so fierce it ripped his specs away, hurling them into the depths.

The view is extensive in every direction, virtually everything that is anything can be spotted. Notable exceptions are High Street, Coniston Old Man and Pillar, which are hidden by obtruding fells. This summit is a good spot for spending time studying your map and attempting to orientate yourself with Lakeland's superb skyline. Pick a calm day though or your map may join David's specs somewhere in the depths of Coledale.

To descend, continue past the summit cairn, alongside the old wall, to a rusting fence stanchion. The wall turns left near this stanchion, before shortly veering on to the fell's north-east ridge. Follow the easy path alongside the wall and down this grassy ridge eventually to reach a fence at the edge of the forest. Cross the fence by a stile and walk left on to a forest road. Turn right and follow this forest road down to a fork. Turn left, uphill, at the fork. At the next fork turn right and down to cross a bridge over the Sanderson Gill. Climb up the far slope then fork left, then left again, to emerge on to the Whinlatter Pass road. Turn left up the road and across Comb Bridge. Just beyond the bridge a path climbs right through the trees into the Visitor Centre car-park.

THE BUTTERMERE FELLS

Distance 6 miles
3400 feet of ascent

Grasmoor End

When looking from the summit of Mellbreak it would appear that some Norse God once stood on Grasmoor's dome, dug a spade into it, and shovelled off the north-west corner, leaving Grasmoor End, a towering thousand foot pyramid of scree-fan, gully and crumbling crag. Its principal feature is Lorton Gully, a Y-shaped rift that is experienced mountain-scrambler country only. However, for the fell-walker who enjoys easy scrambling through dramatic rock-scenery the northern rim of Grasmoor End offers an enjoyable ascent.

Parking: Lanthwaite Green car park. (GR 159208).

CROSS the road and follow the path climbing gently across Lanthwaite Green towards the V-shaped entrance of Gasgale Gill. Just before the path drops down to the footbridge spanning the Liza Beck turn right up a steep path through the bracken to reach the foot of the scree-fans below the northern corner of Grasmoor End.

The next section of the climb is not as bad as it looks. A rough path up the right-hand edge of the first scree-fan links with a similar path twisting up through the scree and bracken above. Your objective is an obvious rock gateway. Once through this the path improves and the fun starts. The route is obvious, although higher up the path tends to veer left when faced by any rocky obstacle. If you enjoy easy scrambling in exciting situations you will have more fun by keeping right up the rocky airy rim of Grasmoor End. Higher, a ridge crowned by slabby hummocks is followed by steeper rocks leading to the cairn crowning the grassy summit of Grasmoor End – a superb viewpoint.

A short easy climb up a grassy shoulder leads you to the wind shelter and cairns crowning Grasmoor, 2795 feet.

Now follow the directions given in Walk 11, from Grasmoor to Coledale Hause then on over Hopegill Head and Whiteside for a fine finish to your expedition.

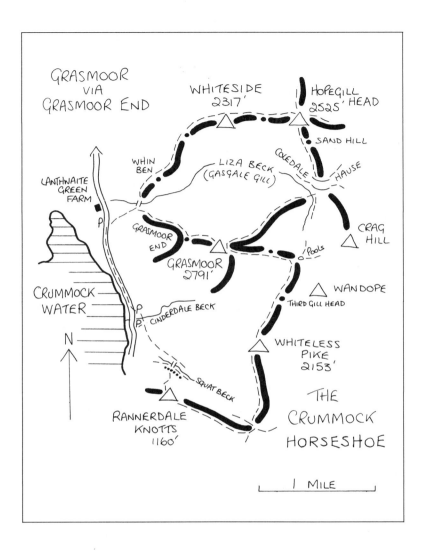

GRASMOOR
VIA
GRASMOOR END

WHITESIDE 2317'

HOPEGILL HEAD 2525'

SAND HILL

WHIN BEN

LIZA BECK
(GASGALE GILL)

COLEDALE HAUSE

CRAG HILL

LANTHWAITE GREEN FARM

P

GRASMOOR END

GRASMOOR 2791'

Pools

WANDOPE

THIRD GILL HEAD

CRUMMOCK WATER

N

P
P   CINDERDALE BECK

WHITELESS PIKE 2153'

SQUAT BECK

THE CRUMMOCK HORSESHOE

RANNERDALE KNOTTS 1160'

1 MILE

The Crummock Horseshoe

Crummock Water is swollen by the becks and gills spilling down the stony pleats of Grasmoor and the shapely fells clustered around it. A traverse of these tops gives a walk of quality. A splendid mix of turfy 'spring-in-the-heels' domes, airy rock-encrusted ridges, and 'mind-blowing' views.

Parking: In either of the two car-parks on Cinderdale Common, (GR 163194). If parked in the car-park signposted 'Cinderdale Car Park', near a litter bin and a 'Footpath' fingerpost, follow this footpath, heading out of the back of the car-park over the common and across Cinderdale Beck. If parked in the smaller car-park at the foot of Cinderdale Beck walk up the right bank to join the previously described path where it crosses the beck and turn right.

FOLLOW a path which passes below a rounded, tree-crowned crag and heads towards the narrow mouth of Rannerdale, dominated by the craggy cone of Rannerdale Knotts. In the valley mouth turn right across a footbridge spanning Squat Beck then climb a stile over a wall. Now climb the steep rough fellside immediately above eventually to emerge onto the summit of Rannerdale Knotts, 1164 feet. (It's the toughest climb on the walk and if you don't fancy it so early after breakfast turn left and follow the path up to the narrow saddle at the head of Rannerdale.)

The views are worth the effort and by the time you have had your fill of them your heart should have stopped trying to fight its way out through your ribcage. Crummock Water lies below, north-westerly gleams Loweswater, and far beyond the Vale of Lorton darkly rise the hills of southern Scotland. Turn and beyond its namesake village glitters Buttermere, piled around with splendid fells, with Gable's high dome looming over the knobbly crest of Hay Stacks.

Now scramble across the rocky hummocks crowning the crest of Rannerdale Knotts and along the grassy ridge beyond to the narrow saddle at the head of Rannerdale. Legend has it that the medieval fellsman defenders of Buttermere lured an invading Norman army into Rannerdale to ambush and slaughter. Nicholas Size, formerly mine host at the Bridge Hotel, wrote a 'factional' but interesting book called *The Secret Valley* which purported to describe the military campaign leading to the bloody finale under Rannerdale Knotts. Novelists Rosemary Sutcliff and Joyce Reason wove their exciting *The Shield Ring* and *The Secret Fortress* around the legend.

Hard facts to support the legend are scarce. Eleventh Century Cumberland was a 'debatable' land, claimed by both English and Scottish Kings. It's a grand tale though, appealing to the romantics among us. The derivation of 'Rannerdale' is 'valley of ravens'. Is this another clue about the legendary battle? In medieval ballads, ravens were birds of evil, flesh eaters who thronged to the place of slaughter.

From the narrow saddle climb the steep twisting path up the far slope, which eases, then steepens again, before you puff up to the cairn crowning Whiteless Pike, 2153 feet. As you step up to the cairn you can see beyond into the deep valley of the Sail Beck, guarded by the grassy blade of the Ard Crags-Knott Rigg ridge and the jutting shaly spurs of Wandope and Crag Hill.

Descend into the dip beyond and on up Whiteless Edge to the cairn crowning Third Gill Head. Walk past the cairn and follow the path curving leftwards above the fell rim on to the grassy saddle dividing Grasmoor from Crag Hill. Here, by some tiny pools marked 722 metres on the relevant 2½″ map, turn left and climb a worn path to a cairn. Continue, cutting across the rim of Grasmoor's steep shaly south flank and over a short rise to shortly reach the cairns and sprawling wind shelter crowning the 2795 foot summit. Walk the few steps to the fell rim to gaze down upon the glittering lakes, set in a ring of fells that time and weather have carved and polished to a rare finish. From your 'birds-eye' viewpoint it's easy to imagine how in the eleventh century it truly would be a 'Secret Fortress'.

Given a clear day now walk north-easterly across the springy turf shortly to find yourself on the airy rim of Dove Crags. Bear right, along the rim and above the steep shaly gullies and ram-shackle pinnacles. Across Gasgale Gill, Whiteside's eroded gullies slash through the pallid buttresses and spew forth the ashen scree that give the fell its name. Beyond the Dove Crags rim, a faint path flanks across a more amenable fellside and down on to a rock-strewn spur which ends above a waterfall in the Liza Beck, where it spills from the grassy upland valley dividing Grasmoor from Crag Hill. Cross the beck and turn down the path on the far bank which leads on to the broad, grassy, and somewhat squelchy, saddle of Coledale Hause. (Given 'white-out' conditions on the summit of Grasmoor it would be wise to disregard the directions given above and return by the way-of-ascent to the pools at 722 metres. Turn left here and descend to Coledale Hause by the path down the 'upland valley'.)

Coledale Hause offers an 'escape route' should you desire it. Simply turn left and follow the path alongside the Liza Beck and down Gasgale Gill to reach the road. Otherwise, climb just west-of-north across steepish grass and scree to reach the cairn crowning the grassy spur called Sand Hill. A grassy dip beyond leads on to the airy rock perch that's the summit of Hopegill Head, 2526 feet. (See Walk 9 for views and natural history interest.)

Descend west, left, down a slender rocky ridge which steepens abruptly into a dip. In wet conditions take care because the slaty rock becomes greasy. Climb on to the broader ridge of Whiteside. The path has a tendency to take the easy line below the crest. This is a pity because it actually ignores the 2358 foot central top, a grassy tor crowned by a midget cairn, which is the true summit of the fell. So keep to the crest, 'bag' the summit and enjoy the sensational views down into Gasgale Gill. From the western cairn a path follows the fell rim down, with a short climb over Whin-Ben, to a footbridge across the Liza Beck. Cross the bridge, climb the far bank and follow a path across Lanthwaite Green, under the crags and gullies of Grasmoor End, (see Walk 10), to reach the road near a car-park. Turn left along the road to reach your car.

A Different Mosedale Horseshoe

This Mosedale Horseshoe should not be confused with the popular Mosedale Horseshoe whose highest peak is Pillar Mountain. It may lack the glamour of its namesake but it offers energetic walking, views that are as equally lovely and varied, and a visit to Lakeland's highest waterfall. It offers a particularly inviting bonus that its more glamourous counterpart cannot match, summits that are relatively uncrowded.

Parking: In the National Trust car-park in Lanthwaite Wood, near Scalehill Bridge, on the road between Lorton and Loweswater. (GR 149215).

WALK back on to the road and over the bridge. Ignore the first fork left and continue on to where the road forks by a telephone box. Mellbreak towers ahead, an exciting challenge. Beyond the hedge and meadows to your left, Crummock Water glimmers and Gable's far dome crowns the head of the 'Secret Fortress' (see Walk 11). Turn left at the telephone box and down past the church to a junction. Turn down left then almost immediately right – 'No Through Road' – to pass behind the Kirkstile Inn. After crossing a bridge over the Park Beck the tarmac ends at Kirkgate Farm. Continue up the rough walled lane. When the lane turns right look back at the towering cone of Grasmoor End, slashed deep by the Y-shaped Lorton Gully. When the lane turns left again look over the wall on your right to see a 'lumpy' field. This is the site of ancient earthworks which look more impressive when seen from high on Mellbreak's northern prow. The lane ends at a gate where paths fork.

Climb left between trees to emerge on to the open fellside. Follow a path up through the bracken to a cairn at the foot of the looming mass of rock, heather and scree. Pause for a 'breather' and a look back at Loweswater gleaming in its wooded hollow. Beyond, the hills of lowland Scotland may be visible rising above the Solway Firth. Now climb a path slanting left over pinky scree. Serpentine steeply up through scree fans and heather banks to the left of an eroded shaly groove. A final slant left leads to an obvious rock pinnacle on the skyline. Turn the pinnacle on its left and climb a rocky ridge to a cairn. Turn left and climb through steep heather on to a ridge. Here, a path forks left on to a ledge giving a surprise view of fiord-like Crummock Water and Buttermere that makes the climb worth every accelerated heartbeat. Step back

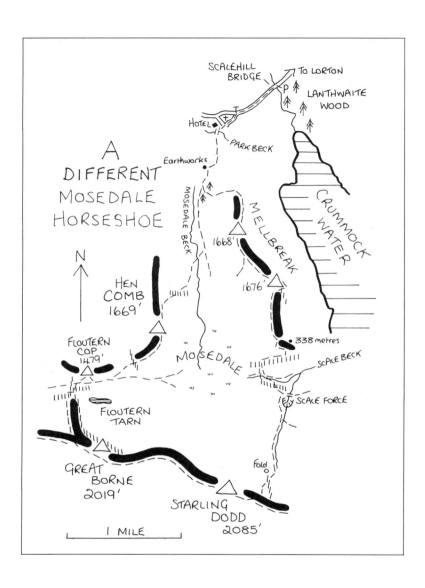

A
DIFFERENT
MOSEDALE
HORSESHOE

N

SCALEHILL
BRIDGE

TO LORTON

P

LANTHWAITE
WOOD

HOTEL

PARK BECK

Earthworks

MOSEDALE BECK

CRUMMOCK WATER

MELLBREAK

1668'

1676'

HEN
COMB
1669'

FLOUTERN
COP
1479'

MOSEDALE

338 metres

SCALE BECK

SCALE FORCE

FLOUTERN
TARN

Fold

GREAT
BORNE
2019'

STARLING
DODD
2085'

1 MILE

on to the ridge path and climb gradually-easing grass slopes to reach the cairns crowning the surprisingly broad northern summit of Mellbreak.

South-easterly, above and beyond the fell's equally brawny southern, and slightly higher top, rises High Stile, with conical Red Pike to its right. Behind Red Pike peeks Pillar. To the left of High Stile looms Gable, the V-gash of Windy Gap, and Green Gable. Below and to the left of Gable, Hay Stacks and Fleetwith Pike curve around the headwaters of Buttermere. Walk a little way east of the cairns for the view down on to Crummock Water, dominated by the massive pinky-grey dome of Grasmoor.

Descend a cairned path to the boggy saddle below the south summit. When this path veers right, fork left along a fainter path which twists and turns up to the cairn at 1679 feet. As you climb look right, between Great Borne and Hen Comb, for a possible glimpse of the Isle of Man. Momentarily, ignore the path heading south from the cairn and walk left to the fell rim for a 'birds-eye' view of Crummock Water and Buttermere.

Walk right, along the rim, between old fence posts, to rejoin the path and follow it steeply down into the hollow below the hillock marked 338 metres on the 2½" map. Go to the right of the hillock, then left above a hollow, to cross a rise beyond and shortly reach a fence. Turn right and follow the fence to a stile. Cross the stile and descend alongside a fence to a crossing path above Black Beck. Cross this path, and the beck, and climb left up the far slope to a fence. Cross this then follow it leftwards across the fellside to the footbridge spanning Scale Beck below the mouth of the gloomy vegetated cleft enfolding Scale Force. If the flow of water allows it, for the best view of the cascade, enter the ravine and scramble up a prominent rib of pinky rock close under its left wall to reach the foot of the 125 foot waterfall, Lakeland's highest.

Emerge from the ravine and climb the path up its right bank. This eventually all but disappears but carry on up Scale Beck to its source. Hereabouts, look for a sheepfold and the rusting posts of an old boundary fence. Climb diagonally right from these to emerge on to the grassy saddle between Little Dodd and Starling Dodd. Turn right and make the short climb to the cairn crowning Starling Dodd, 2076 feet. South-easterly, jutting over the regimented conifers of Ennerdale, in a splendid array of crag, gill, and hanging valley, are Gable, Kirkfell, Pillar, Scoatfell, and Haycock. Westwards, in mellow contrast, lie Ennerdale Water and the patchwork fields of West Cumberland.

A north-westerly dip is followed by a westerly climb up on to the stony, fence-split double-top of Great Borne, 2020 feet. A trig-point crowns the southern and highest summit. Return to the fence and walk left, then right, alongside it before descending steep grass on to a boggy saddle. Here, climb right, then left, over stiles to join the bridleway linking Ennerdale and Buttermere. Turn right along this then almost immediately climb left to 'bag' the grassy cone of Floutern Cop, 1479 feet. Southwards, drab Floutern Tarn lies in a craggy hollow under Great Borne. Now descend east-north-easterly on to a grassy saddle below Hen Comb, before commencing the steep climb, crossing a fence en-route, to the cairn, decorated with an old fencepost, crowning this shapely 1669 foot summit. Descend north-easterly into Mosedale, crossing fences and the Mosedale Beck, to join the bridleway on its far bank which is followed down to a junction with your outward route.

**Distance 7 miles
2600 feet of ascent
OR Distance 10 miles
4200 feet of ascent**

The Buttermere Fells

Walk over Red Pike, High Stile and High Crag and you will have enjoyed a 'classic' Lakeland ridge walk. Springy turf with enough rock bursting through to give it a high mountain flavour, and subtly shifting glimpses of lake, tarn and combe-dimpled fell. Add Hay Stacks and Fleetwith Pike and although your knees might complain your eyes will delight in the bonus of views, and your peak-bagger's soul in the bonus of tops.

Parking: The car park to the right (behind) of the Fish Hotel, Buttermere. (GR 174169.)

TURN RIGHT in front of the Fish Hotel, then right again past the hotel car park, on to a fenced path. Follow this path across the fields, ignoring a right fork signposted 'Scale Bridge/Scale Force', towards the silvery thread of Sour Milk Gill spilling down the wooded flank of Red Pike. A footbridge takes you over Buttermere Dubs, the beck linking Buttermere with Crummock Water. Then a 'Red Pike' sign points left to a smaller footbridge, followed by a kissing-gate between a wall and fence at the edge of the lake. Beyond this a path twists up onto a crossing path in the woods signposted 'Red Pike/Lakeshore'.

Climb the recently rebuilt 'Red Pike' path slanting leftwards through the trees. A vast improvement on the formerly eroded trough, it slants left then right up the steep rocky fellside above the tree-line. The angle eases as it passes through an old wall and a threadbare line of ancient trees to reach the bank of Sour Milk Gill which is followed to emerge on to the shore of Bleaberry Tarn. Bleaberry Combe is yet another of Lakeland's elegantly sculpted hanging valleys whose beauty is enhanced by a tarn. It is marred only by the badly eroded path slashing like an open wound the breast of Red Pike. We who love the high fells are in danger of loving them to death. Scramble up its shaly grooves, ultimately to emerge by the cairn crowning Red Pike, 2479 feet. Five lakes, Ennerdale Water, Crummock Water, Loweswater, Buttermere and Derwentwater can be glimpsed. Some years ago, on an exceptionally clear day, Ben Lomond was spotted from Red Pike, a distance of 120 miles. Across Crummock Water, the Crummock Horseshoe (Walk 11), an interesting jumble of cones, domes and ridges, catches the eye.

Now head on to High Stile. The rusting remains of an old

boundary fence will be met just south of and below the summit of Red Pike. It is nailed all along the undulating spine of these fells and can be a useful aid to navigation in bad weather. Given good weather, keep close to the airy north-east rim of these fells for the 'birds-eye' views of tarn and lakes, often framed between the rock walls of gullies. A pleasant walk leads around the rim of Bleaberry Combe and up on to the bouldery summit of High Stile, 2644 feet. En route the rock changes from the pinky granite, or granophyre, which gives Red Pike its name, to the greyer and more familiar Borrowdale volcanic.

According to the cartographer the true summit of High Stile is the cairn on the north-eastern spur, splitting Bleaberry from Birkness (Burtness) Combe, which is one metre higher than the cairned eminence crowning the rim of Chapel Crags, above Bleaberry Combe. West-south-westerly, beyond the head of Ennerdale Water, the Isle of Man may be spotted floating above the summit of Lank Rigg. Due south, Pillar stands proudly above the monotonous carpet of Ennerdale conifers. Try to pick out the famous Pillar Rock, tucked close under the fell's flattish summit.

Descend alongside the old fence, south at first, then swinging south-easterly around the rim of Birkness Combe, ultimately to surmount the grassy summit of High Crag, 2443 feet. Birkness Combe is not graced by a tarn but lined with magnificent crags which endow it with a special wild beauty. This is climber's country, from the dank overhangs of Eagle Crag to the sunnier slabs of Grey Crags. Every fellwalker worth his or her salt should make an effort to climb up into this delectable corrie – one of Lakeland's finest.

By the time you've reached High Crag top, Gable's proud dome and its pointy underling Green Gable must be a familiar sight. Marching rightwards of them, above and beyond brawny 'table mountain' Kirkfell, are Ill Crag, Broad Crag, Scafell Pike and Scafell – three thousand footers all. Descend south-easterly, still passing the occasional fencepost, down the steep and badly eroded scree and grass slope of Gamlin End. A tiny nameless tarn lies at the foot of this slope. If you visit in May, you could find its surface carpeted with the lovely pink and white Bogbean. Should your knees have gone on strike after the hellish descent of Gamlin End turn left, over the fell rim, and follow a path alongside a wall, eventually to join the Scarth Gap path where it passes through the wall. Turn left down this path, ultimately to join the path bearing left along the lakeshore. Beyond the footbridge over Comb Beck, spilling out of Birkness Combe, the path forks. Follow the right fork along the shoreline into the woods for a delightful lakeside finish to your day. This path is particularly enjoyable on a clear late winter afternoon, or a summer evening, with the Grasmoor fells, gilded with sun and brushed with shadow, rising above and reflected in the limpid water.

Hay Stacks and Fleetwith Pike

IF you are still 'rarin' to go' when you reach the foot of Gamlin End, continue along the ridge, over the rocky crest of Seat, and down a steep rocky path on to the high saddle of Scarth Gap. Scarth Gap was a vital link in the net of ancient highways draped across the Lakeland fells. Travellers, merchants, itinerant workers, monks, soldiers on leave, smugglers, all passed this way long, long before the fells 'were a twinkle in Wainright's eye'.

Cross the pass and climb the well-worn path up the far slope on to the rocky crest above. Pleasant scrambling over, or around, the rocky humps, nailed here and there by rusting fenceposts, leads to a rocky hollow enfolding a small tarn. Rising beyond is a rocky ridge crowned by a cairn at either end. The right-hand cairn appears to be the highest, and the 1958 foot summit of Hay Stacks.

The summit tarn has no name but is sometimes mistakenly called Innominate Tarn, which means 'tarn with no name'. The proper Innominate Tarn, however, is the next, and larger, tarn along the ridge. So we sometimes have a situation where the tarn which truly has no name is called 'the tarn with no name' which leaves the tarn which is truly called 'the tarn with no name' without a name. Are you still with me?

The high mountain tarns are perhaps the loveliest of the jewels in Lakeland's scenic crown. The word 'tarn' is derived from the Old Norse 'tjorn', meaning 'tear'. Tucked among Hay Stacks' stony hummocks are some of the loveliest 'tears of the mountains'. The encircling higher peaks ensure that the views from Hay Stacks are intimate rather than panoramic, though absorbing for all that. See if you can pick out the thin scrawl upon the massive flank of Pillar which is the popular High Level Route to Pillar Rock.

Descend beyond the cairn and follow the worn path south-easterly, behind the rocky hummocks guarding the big crags falling into Warnscale Bottom, down to the shore of Innominate (enough said) Tarn. Pass to the left of the tarn (hereabouts the ubiquitous old fenceposts bid you farewell). Descend, then bear right, under a crag and above a drop giving a fine 'birds-eye' view of Warnscale Bottom and the lakes. Swing left to cross the Black Beck where it spills from the tarn of the same name. Black Beck Tarn is nicely set in a ring of craglets handsomely backclothed with Great Gable and Green Gable.

Climb up to and through a rocky groove, then fork right behind the rocky eminence of Green Crag. The path now passes behind

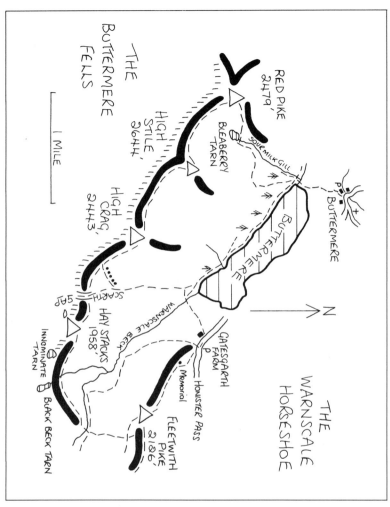

rocky hummocks, with bogs and tarnlets to your right and the elephantine rock mound of Great Round How rising beyond. Beyond the last hummock the path dips right across a beck, then up to and under the steep rocks of Little Round How, before dropping again to cross the Warnscale Beck by stepping stones.

Climb left through the heather to join a better path. This is a former 'slate road' that once serviced Dubs Quarry, just above. It is a convenient 'escape' route back to the valley but it would be a pity, at this stage, not to 'stiffen the sinews and summon up the blood' for the last climb. Head up the heathery fellside. You may stumble upon a crossing path which leads left to the summit of Fleetwith Pike but if you miss the connection don't worry. Keep climbing and you'll eventually find yourself on the edge of a 'gurt hole' up which faintly float the sounds of labouring combustion engines. Go left along the edge of the void to reach the cairn crowning Fleetwith Pike, 2126 feet.

Elsewhere in this book I have described the beautiful fiord-like view of the two lakes seen from Mellbreak. The view from Fleetwith Pike matches it in topography and loveliness but from the opposite direction. From here you can also dwell with satisfaction on the ridges you have traversed and the peaks you have 'bagged' this very day. Descend the steepish narrowish north-westerly ridge, or 'Fleetwith Edge'. Eventually the ridge eases out on to a grassy dip behind the crest of Low Raven Crag. The path drops right to twist steeply down the fellside. This used to be an unpleasant descent over glutinous clayey soil but happily now the path has been reconstructed. As you pass below the crag, look up to see the white memorial cross marking where an unfortunate young Victorian girl lost her life, apparently as a result of tripping over her 'fell-pole'. Fell-poles were the Lakeland equivalent of an alpenstock and 'de riguer' in Victorian fellwalking circles, and even earlier. Before setting out on one of his walking expeditions Coleridge wrestled with his irate wife for her broom handle to use as an improvised fell-pole.

Continue down to the road then turn left down to Gatesgarth Farm. In the early Fifties we used to 'bivouac' in the barn of Gatesgarth Farm. (I remember one occasion when it was my turn to 'cook' the dinner, a huge pan of stew set on a roaring primus. I was lethargically stirring it with a large plastic spoon, gazing through the barn door at the sun-gilded crests and thinking about the rock climbs we had done that day in Birkness Combe. I became aware that the spoon was sliding remarkably easily through the thick stew. Lifting it out I saw there were only about two inches of handle left – the rest had melted! I said 'nowt', and nobody complained, and we're all still around.)

Turn left through the gate signposted 'Public Bridleway – Ennerdale/Buttermere' and follow the path across the fields at the head of the lake. After crossing the footbridge over Warnscale Beck join the lakeshore path as described earlier in the descent from below Gamlin End and follow it back to Buttermere.

Walk 13 could be done equally as well from Gatesgarth Farm as from Buttermere Village.

The Warnscale Horseshoe

It must be fairly obvious from the previous description (Walk 13) that the round of Hay Stacks and Fleetwith Pike would make a short but interesting walk for its own sake.

Parking: The car park opposite Gatesgarth Farm, at the foot of Honister Pass, would be the most convenient. (GR 195151.)

FROM Gatesgarth Farm follow the 'Public Bridleway – Ennerdale/ Buttermere' path across the fields at the head of Buttermere. The Warnscale Horseshoe looms to your left. At the path fork signposted 'Public Bridleway – Ennerdale via Scarth Gap/Buttermere' climb left, following the worn path to Scarth Gap.

From Scarth Gap follow the description in Walk 13, THE CONTINUATION, from 'climb the well-worn path up the far slope on to the rocky crest above –'.

The Buttermere Horseshoe

I realise it's a fanciful notion but it seems to me that Dalehead, Hindscarth, and Robinson turn their backs on Buttermere. As if implying 'We're part of the classic Newlands Horseshoe and nothing to do with you, so there!' Compare the largely grassy whalebacks they present to Buttermere to the steep craggy flanks and spiny ridges they tumble down into Newlands and you'll see what I mean. Add them to Walk 13, however, and they become instead part of the 'Buttermere Horseshoe'. A less publicised but far more arduous undertaking.

Parking: As for Walk 13.

FOLLOW the directions given in Walk 13 as far as the summit of Fleetwith Pike. It must be obvious that should weather, energy, or morale have deteriorated at this point you could continue with Walk 13 back to Buttermere and try again another day.

If not, follow the path, easterly, along the ridge overlooking Honister Crag, to a rough quarry road which leads you down to Honister Pass. Across the road a wood and wire fence climbs the grassy south flank of Dalehead. Dalehead from Honister Pass is perhaps the easiest 'two-thousand footer' in Lakeland. Thousands follow the worn trail alongside the fence and rusting boundary posts that lead to the summit. Yet barely a hop, skip, and a jump away is a far more entertaining route that appears to be totally neglected.

From the foot of the fence, walk left along a gently inclined grassy path. This is a former quarryman's path, now disused, leading to a derelict tramway. Climb up, or alongside, the rusting rails, passing the blocked-off entrances to several 'adits'. Pause for a 'breather' and a look back across the hazy gulf of Honister Pass at the scarred and gouged face of Honister Crag. Until 1914 Honister quarrymen lived, as well as worked, on the mountain, only visiting their families at weekends. Often they communicated by carrier pigeon. The Buttermere Green Slate Company also used this method to pass urgent messages to their Head Office in Keswick. One wonders what effect the passing peregrine falcon had on the sales of slate.

When you reach the end of the rails climb on to find a splendid example of a Drum House, with the rusting cable still coiled around the drum. Trams of slate were winched down the rails to

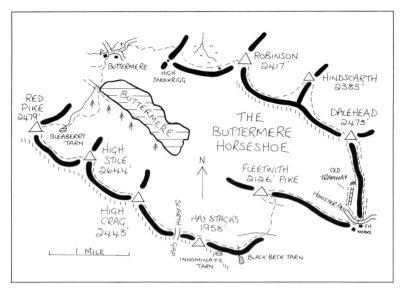

the dressing sheds, and 'empties' hauled back up the fellside. The early quarrymen used to move up to a quarter of a ton of slate on sleds, or 'trailbarrows'; running before them like a horse before laboriously hauling the empty sleds back uphill. One Honister man, Joseph Clarke of Stonethwaite, is recorded as having shifted five tons of slate in seventeen journeys.

Climb on to reach a derelict workshop on a grassy shelf and splendid viewpoint. From here, climb right and scramble across the neck of a derelict quarry. Continue right across the fellside to meet the fence accompanying the 'tourist' path. Follow this path to the handsome cairn crowning the summit of Dalehead.

Now follow the directions given in Walk 1 from – 'Descend just north of west along the fell rim' to 'the Isle of Man thrusting over the shoulder of Red Pike'. From the Robinson cairn, descend west-south-westerly down a steepening path to a cairn. The angle eases now and the path follows a west to north-westerly curve around the swampy rim of Buttermere Moss. After passing to the right of the subsidiary summit of High Snockrigg look for a path dropping left down a grassy groove. Follow this path which twists down to join the road leading down into Buttermere Village.

MARATHON

Walk 16

Distance 24 miles
9000 feet of ascent

The Ennerdale Horseshoe

Although it's only partially inside the boundaries of this guidebook I couldn't resist including this challenging walk. It's a tough one and rightfully earns a place in that splendid mountain-walkers 'coffee-table' book 'The Big Walks'. Although it requires a higher degree of determination and energy than any other walk described in this book you don't have to be a superman/woman in order to walk it – if you're feeling reasonably fit, have a go. It's an experience you'll never forget!

Parking: The Ennerdale Forest car park near the bridge over the River Ehen. (GR 085154).

CROSS the bridge and walk left along the far bank to re-cross the river by a footbridge. Walk along the lakeshore eventually passing a grassy car park at 094161. Shortly, just beyond a gate, turn left to cross a stile then climb, first to the left and then to the right of a wall/fence to emerge on to a road near Whins Farm. Walk right to a junction then follow the 'Public Bridleway' on to the open fell. Obey the access signs and adhere to the bridleway until you reach the saddle between Floutern Cop and Great Borne. Now climb steeply right alongside the fence onto the summit of Great Borne. The sight of Gable, the stony axis of this walk, long miles away, gives you a harsh hint of the task you have set yourself.

A wood and wire fence leads you off Great Borne and towards Starling Dodd. For much of this walk isolated rusting fenceposts and, latterly, a drystone wall, prove useful aids to navigation. Starling Dodd's grassy cone is followed by lowly Little Dodd then a steepish finish up scree on to the aptly named summit of Red Pike.

Easy walking around the rim of Bleaberry Combe, overlooking its lovely tarn, leads to the bouldery summit of High Stile. En route the pink granite, or granophyre, gives way to the more familiar grey Borrowdale volcanic. Similar walking around the rim of Birkness Combe brings you to the grassy summit of High Crag. The fell edge hereabouts is sharper and there are big crags below you. Birkness Combe is climber's country.

Beyond High Crag the steep, badly eroded Gamlin End flank leads painfully down to a grassy saddle. Seat now blocks the ridge, a rocky hiccup that frustratingly demands its toll of energy before Scarth Gap is reached.

Hay Stacks, the next challenge is in a class of its own. Given thick mist this lowly fell requires thoughtful navigation and the old fenceposts are a definite asset hereabouts.

I found the long grind up Brandreth particularly exhausting. My morale wasn't helped when I was nearly trampled underfoot by a phalanx of fellrunners as I staggered up to the cairn. From Brandreth, a stony and eroded 'trod' leads over Green Gable and down into Windy Gap. Gable's bouldery dome is then surmounted by a steepish climb up slabby rocks polished smooth by a trillion pairs of boots.

Reaching Gable top gives you a psychological boost for now you can say you are on the way 'home'. It's best however, to say this with your eyes shut for if you look too closely 'home' is a very long way away!

A knee-jellying, scree-slithery plunge north-westerly leads onto the saddle of Beckhead. The ubiquitous fenceposts then lead you over Kirkfell's twin tarn-divided summits and down the fell's steep rocky northern corner onto Black Sail Pass. Kirkfell is a superb viewpoint. Gable makes the hairs on your neck bristle, and the Scafells are cleft and cragged in a manner befitting England's rooftree.

The long climb over Looking Stead and up the south-east ridge of Pillar is a hard slog at this stage of the walk. First time visitors to Pillar's table-like summit should walk to the Ennerdale rim for an exciting glimpse of Pillar Rock. (A more interesting alternative would be to climb Pillar by its craggy Ennerdale flank along the popular High Level Route. This route would require considerably more energy however, so don't choose it if you've little to spare. I hadn't, so I didn't!)

From Pillar a steep rocky ridge descends south-westerly into Wind Gap. A steep bouldery climb up the far slope leads to the cairn crowning Black Crag. A pleasant grassy ridge follows, with the isolated high combes of Blackem Head and Mirklin Cove to either hand. A short, bouldery scramble leads to the summit of Scoatfell, whose tiny cairn is balanced on top of the drystone wall which will now accompany you for most of your homeward trek. North of Scoatfell rises Steeple's craggy cone. Bag it if you wish, and have the time and energy to spare. Don't feel guilty if you don't because it is only a spur off the main ridge, albeit an enticing one. I didn't, and don't!

The going becomes nice and turfy now with none of those nasty rocks that leap up and stub aching feet. Haycock proves a short, steep, but painful climb at this stage of the game. A swing north-westerly crosses the rocky hiccup of Little Gowder Crag, beyond which ridge and wall veer west again on to the broad grassy summit of Caw Fell. From here the wall swings abruptly north, down on to a grassy saddle before beginning the long, it seemed interminable to me, haul over Iron Crag, the last of the two-thousand footers. To seaward the cooling towers of Sellafield bring a touch of menace to a view which, on a clear evening, encompasses the hills of Galloway, the Isle of Man and, peeping over the far horizon between them, the hills of Ulster.

At Black Pots, the saddle beyond Iron Crag, go through a gate and up a gap in the trees on to a forest track. Turn left keeping your eyes open for a cairn on your right. Turn right at the cairn and follow a path through trees, over a stile, and on in wobbly-kneed triumph to the summit of Crag Fell. Descend a steep path to cross Ben Gill above where it spills into a rocky ravine. When you see a gate ahead turn right down a stony zig-zag path to the foot of the ravine then follow the gill down to a crossing path. Turn left along the edge of the forest to where a stile, just beyond Crag Farm House, leads you down to journeys end.